Click on this link to receive an introduction to the 10 critical skills that we need to develop to empower our learning and development of situational awareness. You will also have access to learn more about our Situational Awareness Programs and how you can enroll to learn this critical skill to Make Yourself and Your Family Safe.

https://aha.pub/10SafetySkills

Prepare for the Real World

The World Is Not A Safe Place

Brian Searcy

Foreword by Jeff Hoffman

An Actionable Business Journal

E-mail: info@thinkaha.com
20660 Stevens Creek Blvd., Suite 210
Cupertino, CA 95014

Published by THiNKaha®
20660 Stevens Creek Blvd., Suite 210,
Cupertino, CA 95014
https://thinkaha.com
E-mail: info@thinkaha.com

THiNK**aha**

First Printing: March 2022
Hardcover ISBN: 978-1-61699-393-1 1-61699-393-6
Paperback ISBN: 978-1-61699-392-4 1-61699-392-8
eBook ISBN: 978-1-61699-391-7 1-61699-391-X
Place of Publication: Silicon Valley, California, USA
Paperback Library of Congress Number: 2022900010

Dedication

I would like to dedicate this book to three people.

The first is my beautiful, intelligent, and successful wife, Heather Searcy. She is my rock and has supported and empowered me on our mission to educate everyone on the need for Situational Awareness.

The second person is Mark Stratton. Mark is with the Lord today. A gifted and talented entrepreneur, we started a company years ago called *Main Street Pilot*. Our mission was to develop a Micro e-Learning Program that would allow for the learning of Personal Skills. The work we did together before his death lives on in this book and the Paratus Group *Prepare for the Real World Programs*.

The third person is Jeff Hoffman. Jeff Hoffman, an award-winning global entrepreneur, proven CEO, worldwide motivational speaker, bestselling author, Hollywood film producer, a producer of a Grammy Award-winning jazz album, and executive producer of an Emmy Award-winning television show, is also a friend and a mentor. I reached out to him with an ask. That ask was to write the foreword for this book. A very busy man on a mission today, he took time out of his schedule to share an amazing story and relate how it ties directly to Situational Awareness and this book.

Acknowledgements

First and foremost, I would like to thank the Lord for the blessings he has bestowed on me and my family. To my wife, Heather, thank you for your undying support as I continue on this mission to educate and train as many people as possible on Situational Awareness.

Putting together a unique program to enable the learning of Situational Awareness has been and continues to be a passion of mine. I know that we all have Situational Awareness—it is a gift given to us by God. It's that instinct, the "hair on the back of the neck" feeling that we get when something isn't right. The problem today is that people don't know that they have it, and if they do know that they have it, they don't trust it and don't know how to act on it.

The development of these programs would not be where they are today without the help of great friends and mentors. To begin, I would also like to thank Jeffery Hayzlett and Tricia Benn for their support and mentorship; Nate Kievman for his guidance and friendship; Col (Ret) Ed "Tank" Mckinzie for his unwavering support; Micah Richardson for his knowledge, expertise, and encouragement; and Maj (Ret) Scott Huesing for his guidance to read *Left of Bang* by Patrick Van Horne and Jason A. Riley.

I would like to thank Dr. Randy Brown and Charlie Mann from Alvord ISD for all their help and patience as we built this program. Much has been learned, and the program continues to improve. I would like to thank Madeline Ross for her encouragement and guidance to improve the program.

Finally, I would like to thank Mitchell Levy and his team. Without their guidance, patience, and support, this book would not have been written.

How to Read a THiNKaha® Book

A Note from the Publisher

The AHAthat/THiNKaha series was crafted to deliver content the way humans process information in today's world—short sweet, and to the point, while delivering powerful, lasting impact.

The content is designed and presented to appeal to visual, auditory, and kinesthetic personality types. Each section contains AHA messages, lines for notes, and a meme that summarizes that section. You should also scan the QR code, or click on the link, to watch a video of the author talking about that section.

This book is contextual in nature. Although the words won't change, their meaning will every time you read it as your context will. Be ready, you will experience your own AHA moments as you read. The AHA messages are designed to be stand-alone actionable messages that will help you think differently. Items to consider as you're reading include:

1. It should only take less than an hour to read the first time. When you're reading, write one to three action items that resonate with you in the underlined areas.
2. Mark your calendar to re-read it again.
3. Repeat step #1 and mark one to three additional AHA messages that resonate. As they will most likely be different, this is a great time to reflect on the messages that resonated with you during your last reading.
4. Sprinkle credust on the author and yourself by sharing the AHA messages from this book socially from the AHAthat platform https://aha.pub/SituationalAwareness.

After reading this THiNKaha book, marking your AHA messages, rereading it, and marking more AHA messages, you'll begin to see how this book contextually applies to you. We advocate for continuous, lifelong learning, and this book will help you transform your AHAs into action items with tangible results.

Mitchell Levy, Global Credibility Expert
publisher@thinkaha.com

A THiNKaha book is not your typical book. It's a whole lot more, while being a whole lot less. Scan the QR code or use this link to watch me talk about this new evolutionary style of book: https://aha.pub/THiNKahaSeries

Contents

Foreword by Jeff Hoffman

I want to talk about the importance of situational awareness in the office, a place where most of us do not think about situational awareness because we in business tend to believe we already know everything about our situation since it's our office. It's the same office we come into every day with the same people while seeing the same thing. Therefore, we don't really think about situational awareness because it's like we wonder, "What do I need to be aware of?"

However, I want to share how I became tipped off to the fact that I needed to dramatically pay attention to situational awareness at work to improve efficiency, success, profitability, and everything about my company.

I was visiting another company with another CEO, and their growth rate was phenomenal. Their company was killing it every year—explosive growth and getting increasingly bigger, and I asked him the questions: What is it you're doing that everybody else isn't? Why is your business growth so powerful?

He said, "Jeff, let me show you. Let me show you what goes on in my office that probably doesn't go on in most offices."

They had written the fundamental reasons they come into work every day on the wall.

For example, if you're in the travel business or the hotel business, what would be written on the wall is: Book another hotel room. Therefore, the only reason you're in that office is to book a hotel room.

He had written this on the wall, and he said, "First of all, the fundamental reason we're in this office every day is written on the wall, so at all times when you're in this office, you are always aware of the reason we come to work every day. We're just here to get someone in a hotel room, and it was written on the wall. It struck me that since it's so easy to get distracted at work, that's a visual reminder of the situation we're in."

Something that makes everybody aware of why we come to work every day was a great idea. First, you have that written on the wall, and then he showed me something. He said, "Walk with me."

We walked down the hall, and we ran into a woman that works for his company. He asked her, "What are you working on right now?" She answered, and he pointed at the wall and said, "How does that help us achieve this goal, the reason we're here every day?" He told me that there are only two answers. Either she can explain why she'll achieve the tasks she's doing right now—I'll stick with my example of selling another hotel room—or he tells her to put it down and do something else.

So, every day, there is an innate awareness of what they're at work to do, what they are working on right now, at any moment, and how to achieve that goal. He even showed me that when he, as a CEO, asks an employee to do something, they have the right to say to him, "I'm not sure how that is helping achieve the goal on the wall, so I'm going to say no." I was very inspired because it was a very aware company.

Every day, they knew why they were there, their situation, their tasks, and how these contributed to what they were trying to get done.

So, I went back to my office and wrote on the wall why we were here every day. Sell rooms in a hotel. When I started talking to my employees, I realized that our situational awareness was low.

I have asked many people to tell me what they were working on, but they did not know how the job the company had assigned them would us achieve our goal.

So, I went to my conference room and created a chart on the wall. On the chart, I wrote our company's goals, and under the goals, I wrote the objectives, meaning how we are going to achieve those goals. If your goal was to sell a million hotel rooms, your objective would be to sell 200,000 on the West Coast, 100,000 in the Midwest, etc. I wrote those objectives. I wrote a strategy for achieving our West Coast sales numbers, and I wrote the tactics underneath that.

What approach would we take to implement those strategies? Under that, I wrote tasks—the actual tasks. When someone walks into the office, what do we need them to do to achieve those tactics, to support those strategies that achieve our objectives that lead to our goal? Underneath the tasks, I wrote the skills you need to achieve those tasks.

I called my entire company into the office. I wanted to create situational awareness, so I dramatically said, "I have good and bad news."

I said, "The bad news is effective right now; all 40 of you are fired!"

Everybody groaned, and I said, "But there's good news. The good news is I'm starting a brand-new company right now, and I need 40 employees who want a job." When I asked who was interested, all 40 hands went up. Then I said, "Here's what you have to do to get a job at the new company.

"Take this marker, walk over to the board, and circle the skills that you have and then from there, the task you will do with those skills, followed by the tactics, the support, the strategies, the objectives, all the way up to how the work you are doing right this minute—any task you do in any skill you have. How are you deploying those resources to achieve the goal we came into this office to achieve?

Everybody started circling on this chart. What am I doing? Using what skills? How is it supporting the company's goals to take us where we're going? I realized it completely changed our operational efficiency because it created situational awareness for what we do daily.

Whenever people were in a business situation at work, looking at what they'd be spending their time on, they would say, "How is it going to help us achieve our goals?" Because they were aware, they would look at the board and ask, "How does the work we're discussing help contribute to our goals?"

Our efficiency went up dramatically, and we stopped spending time on things that didn't matter because we came much more acutely aware of what did matter to make our business successful.

Brian Searcy's book is a must-read because we get so caught up in the familiarity of our everyday surroundings that we stop looking any deeper than the surface.

Situational awareness is looking deeper than the surface. It's understanding where you truly are, the results you desire to have, the results you want to prevent, and what steps and skills you need to make those things happen.

This book will teach you the habits of becoming situationally aware, so it becomes second nature to you, instead of the way we operate today, which is just getting so lost in the noise that we're no longer aware of what's going on around us. Deploying situational awareness at your company will dramatically change your success.

Introduction

So happy that you picked up this book. My vision is to "Make You and Your Family Safe by Redefining How Safety is Learned" to make schools, churches, the workplace, our communities, and families as safe as possible.

My unique experience and expertise have revolutionized how situational awareness is learned, allowing everyone in our communities to learn and develop Situational Awareness Habits, Behaviors, and Mindsets.

This is critical to understanding what "Left of Bang" means and how the learning of Situational Awareness empowers you to prevent incidents from happening, ensuring that you and your family are not victims.

Left of Bang.

Left of Bang is the difference between being proactive and preventing bad things from happening, with having to respond to a threat that surprises you that you are not prepared for and have no idea how to respond.

The "Bang" is the bad thing happening. It could be an active shooter event, bullying, sexual harassment, suicide, or one of the myriad of other threats we face today. When we say "Left of Bang," we are talking about being empowered to be able to prevent something from happening and keep yourself or someone else from being a victim by recognizing the threat and then actually being able to take an action to prevent it from happening.

Please take a look at my extended bio, which reinforces what gives me the credibility to make the statement above:

Brian Searcy is a proven USAF combat and senior leader. A retired Colonel with over 23 years of honorable service, his leadership career spanned over 20 deployments both as a navigator and leader. He was flying as a navigator on a Saudi AWACS when Iraq invaded Kuwait during the first Gulf War. As a young officer, he was selected to support the AWACS mission on the JSOC Mission Planning Team. He supported Operations Northern and Southern Watch and most of the conflicts our country was involved with over his career. As a Squadron Commander, his airmen were responsible for the operation of the Combat Operations Floor in the Combined Air Operations Center (CAOC), which was tasked with the execution of all air operations in Afghanistan and Iraq. He had two tours at the Pentagon and ended his career as the Vice Wing/Active-Duty Wing Commander for JSTARS.

Following a decorated senior leadership career, Brian transitioned into executive roles as a business entrepreneur, writer, publisher, and public speaker. He co-founded The Paratus Group to use his decades-tested and proven leadership and training experience to solve a need for relevant, effective, trustworthy principles, training methodologies, and programs to allow for the learning of situational awareness.

Brian is an expert contributor appearing on The Fox News Channel, interviews on over 100 national radio stations, and has been on dozens of Podcasts. As a founding flying member of the Joint Surveillance and Target Attack Radar System (JSTARS), Brian was responsible for the development of the doctrine and training executed when the Wing went operational. Years later, he refined the JSTARS operational procedures as the Active-Duty Wing Commander. As a Squadron Commander, his airmen were responsible for developing and testing the doctrine that shaped the future training and operating procedures for the USAF Combined Air Operation Centers (CAOC). Brian is the host and producer of Situational Awareness & Your Safety Podcast, sharing experiences for leaders in education, business, and safety on how important Situational Awareness is to our safety and success.

Brian is a formally trained public speaker with 30 years of experience in the military and private sector. He has spoken to over 5000 audiences conveying his thoughts, intent, and goals to motivate listeners. Brian's knowledge, experiences, and natural outgoing style allows him to connect with audiences to share his experience.

Brian dedicates his time to travel to a multitude of venues to educate on the need to change how we look at the threats we face today in our communities and the need to defeat Einstein's definition of "Insanity" by changing paradigms on how the learning of Situational Awareness needs to take place. He is continually sought out to speak on leadership and expertise on the learning of Situational Awareness.

Brian has been on Fox News, over 100 local and nationally syndicated radio shows, has spoken to the Maryland Center for School Safety, and over 50 Professional Organizations, School Districts, Churches, and Businesses.

Learning and developing #SituationalAwareness enables you to take responsibility for your own safety and for that of your community.

Brian Searcy

https://aha.pub/SituationalAwareness

Share the AHA messages from this book socially by going to
https://aha.pub/SituationalAwareness

Scan the QR code or use this link to watch the section videos and more on this section topic:
https://aha.pub/SituationalAwarenessSVs

Section I

Situational Awareness is a Process To Prevent, Remove and Respond

Less than one in seven people today have situational awareness. This statistic is distressing because it is a gift that we have all been given. But over the last decades, for a number of reasons, people did not learn that they had this critical skill, nor did they learn how to identify it, how to trust it, and then how to act on it.

Instead, do you ever notice how many people's eyes are glued to their phones, completely unaware of their surroundings? This happens almost everywhere. When you do not have situational awareness, you can't identify the potential threats, which means you can't prevent them, and prevention should be our number one priority.

Did you know that you lose fine motor skills when your heartbeat reaches 115 beats per minute? If something bad ever happens (or is already happening), what will your response be? Often, people in these situations are caught off guard and left with few or no options. Because they didn't know what to do or didn't act when they could have, their lives were put in danger. Don't let this happen to you!

The skill of situational awareness will empower you to take responsibility for your safety and that of others. When you know how to identify changes in the behavior of people around you, you can be proactive in resolving any issues or threats you face.

Situational awareness will make a difference at home, in the workplace, and in your community. You can gain the ability to understand and deal with threats by being situationally aware. With situational awareness, you will be able to identify when something isn't right and, more importantly, know what to do if you need to act on it.

This section discusses what situational awareness is and why it's important. You'll learn how situational awareness can ensure your own safety and that of others.

1

#SituationalAwareness is a skill that can help you make effective decisions to ensure your own safety and that of others.

_____

_____

_____

2

The FBI and the Secret Service have stated that 93% of bad things that happen are preventable. #SituationalAwareness

_____

_____

_____

3

Many problems we face in life happen because we either act without thinking or think without acting. #SituationalAwareness

_____

_____

_____

4

#SituationalAwareness can help you prevent something bad from happening, teach you how to remove yourself and others from that situation, and prepare you to respond in such events.

_____

_____

_____

5

#SituationalAwareness can be demonstrated at home and in the workplace. You can develop and hone the ability to identify potential threats that can impact life, wellness, and productivity.

_____

_____

6

In today's society, many people are programmed to simply react. To resolve a potentially dangerous situation, it is better to be proactive.

_____

_____

_____

7

Most people make decisions based on fear or panic.
#SituationalAwareness helps you develop the mindset
necessary to identify and assess problems.

8

You can train the part of your brain associated with
survival instincts to prevent you from experiencing
excessive stress and anxiety. #SituationalAwareness

9

When the hair on your neck stands up, something isn't right. Trust your gut feeling. #SituationalAwareness

_____

_____

_____

10

When faced with a challenging situation, evaluating and analyzing threats helps you predict outcomes and respond accordingly. #SituationalAwareness

_____

_____

_____

11

The definition of insanity is doing the same thing over and over expecting different results. Would you rather wait for someone to solve your problems, or would you rather be #SituationallyAware and solve them yourself?

_____

_____

_____

12

To be #SituationallyAware is to demonstrate leadership by intervening in a potentially dangerous situation.

_____

_____

_____

13

You have a responsibility to make your community as safe as possible. You can't wait for the government or the police to do it. Take action! #SituationalAwareness

_____

_____

_____

14

#SituationalAwareness empowers you to be involved in helping and caring for the safety and well-being of others.

_____

_____

_____

15

Learning and developing #SituationalAwareness enables you to take responsibility for your own safety and for that of your community.

_____

_____

_____

Telling you what to do without providing the skills to execute only results in a false sense of security.
#SituationalAwareness

Brian Searcy

https://aha.pub/SituationalAwareness

Share the AHA messages from this book socially by going to
https://aha.pub/SituationalAwareness

Scan the QR code or use this link to watch the section videos and more on this section topic:
https://aha.pub/SituationalAwarenessSVs

Section II

We Will Not Tell You What to Do

No two situations are alike. Every scenario is unique, so how you act or react should depend on the uniqueness of the scenario you're in. A one-size-fits-all approach is not effective and may cause you and those around you more harm.

There are many traditional "safety" trainings available in the market. For example, you may take training on how to identify active shooters. But if, God forbid, you actually face one, all of your training can easily dissipate. If you don't have situational awareness, you may not be able to think clearly and critically.

Response is personal. Your response in certain situations depends on your perception and capabilities at that particular time. The good news is that you can still develop your physical and emotional strengths over time to be situationally aware.

This section discusses how you can train yourself in making sound (and sometimes split-second) decisions based on who you are, your life experiences, and how you trained your mind and body to respond.

16

No two situations are alike. How you act or react should depend on the uniqueness of the scenario you're in. #SituationalAwareness

_____

_____

_____

17

A one-size-fits-all approach is not effective when in a situation that's life or death and may cause you and those around you more harm. #SituationalAwareness

_____

_____

_____

18

Everyone responds differently to bad situations. We all have different perceptions and perspectives. How you respond is up to you. #SituationalAwareness

_____

_____

_____

19

Your response to any difficult situation is unique to you. It's all a matter of preventing, removing, or responding. #SituationalAwareness

_____

_____

_____

20

Perspective changes everything. How you respond to situations is as unique as you are. #SituationalAwareness

---

21

No two people will behave in the same way under the same circumstances. We all have to learn #SituationalAwareness ourselves.

22

No one can tell you whether you should run, hide, or fight. You must know who you are and what you're capable of to figure that out. #SituationalAwareness

_____

_____

_____

23

General Patton once said, "Never tell people how to do things. Tell them what to do and they will surprise you with their ingenuity." #SituationalAwareness

_____

_____

_____

24

You can't expect good results if you don't have
the necessary skills to respond effectively.
#SituationalAwareness

_____

_____

_____

25

There is no one-size-fits-all. Everyone has different
knowledge, experiences, and capabilities.
#SituationalAwareness

_____

_____

_____

26

Telling you what to do without providing the skills
to execute only results in a false sense of security.
#SituationalAwareness

_____

_____

_____

27

Ten people will respond to the same situation in ten
different ways. You can learn to react in a way that is
practiced and automatic. #SituationalAwareness

_____

_____

_____

28

A mindset that says, "I'll do what Colonel Searcy says I should do," is worthless. The situation could be over before you remember what you were told to do. #SituationalAwareness

_____

_____

_____

29

You need to develop a process of responding on your own capabilities and library of knowledge. #SituationalAwareness

_____

_____

_____

30

You need to own the process of #SituationalAwareness. Consider the myriad things that could happen and how you would respond.

_____

_____

_____

31

#SituationalAwareness is one component that will be helpful as society changes and hopefully becomes more humane.

_____

_____

_____

32

Are you prepared to get involved and intervene? What
can you do with the skills and training you have?
#SituationalAwareness

_____

_____

_____

33

Learning #SituationalAwareness empowers you with the
desire and skills to identify threats and act.

_____

_____

_____

Your goal is to be as proactive as possible when dealing with various #threats, whether physical, psychological, emotional, or some combination thereof.

Brian Searcy

https://aha.pub/SituationalAwareness

Share the AHA messages from this book socially by going to
https://aha.pub/SituationalAwareness

Scan the QR code or use this link to watch the section videos and more on this section topic:
https://aha.pub/SituationalAwarenessSVs

Section III

There Are A Lot of Threats, According to the FBI

Any threat can be prevented if action is taken. Therefore, it's important for you to be educated. You need to know the indicators that could increase the likelihood of impending danger. Developing situational awareness is the key.

You need to understand threats and be able to act on them. This understanding can make a difference when it comes to your safety and that of your family, friends, students, employees, and your community.

Being aware of and identifying threats makes an impact on your mental health and wellness. Having this skill can empower you to lead and de-escalate any problems you encounter at any time of day.

This section presents a few examples of threats. However, the intent of this section is not to merely list all kinds of threats but to become more educated and familiar with all possible scenarios.

In doing so, we can continuously reinforce this knowledge about threats and apply the skill of situational awareness so it becomes natural for us at home, in the workplace, and in our communities.

34

#Threats are everywhere but can be prevented. The first step is knowing what they are and raising awareness among family, colleagues, and the community. #SituationalAwareness

_____

_____

_____

35

Any threat can be prevented if action is taken. Therefore, it's important for you to be educated to decrease the likelihood of being in danger. Developing #SituationalAwareness is the key.

_____

_____

_____

36

Educating ourselves about existing #Threats and how to act on them can make a difference everywhere we go. #SituationalAwareness

_____

_____

_____

37

COVID-19 has become a #Threat, as it has dramatically changed people's lives. Relationship strain, child abuse, depression, and anxiety are on the rise. #SituationalAwareness

_____

_____

_____

38

Human trafficking can take the form of adopting children or luring them through social media with promises of a better life. #SituationalAwareness

_____

_____

_____

39

Examples of #Threats include abduction, active shooters, bullying, and sexual harassment. These can be physical threats or threats to people's psyche, mental health, and overall wellness. #SituationalAwareness

_____

_____

_____

40

Drug abuse, alcoholism, and suicidal tendencies are #Threats. Developing #SituationalAwareness can help you better understand the root causes and how to act on them.

41

When you develop #SituationalAwareness, you learn to pay attention to the goings-on at home, with your kids and spouse, and when they're with friends. #Threats

---

42

You can create learning opportunities at home to help your children develop the mindset and character necessary when faced with #Threats. #SituationalAwareness

_____

_____

_____

43

How can you develop #SituationalAwareness at home? Start by promoting open communication about #Threats and how to act on them.

_____

_____

_____

44

With sexual harassment, the impact can be physical, mental, and emotional. The impact on a person's well-being from only one #Threat can be massive. #SituationalAwareness

_____

_____

_____

45

A large number of active shooters were bullied at some point in their lives. This is a good example of someone who may have tried to get help but felt no one was there. #Threats #SituationalAwareness

_____

_____

_____

46

The suicide rate among teens is rising. This could mean that traditional ways of dealing with these #Threats no longer work. #SituationalAwareness

_____

_____

_____

47

Identifying changes in behavior early can make a difference. You can determine whether someone is going through a phase or if it's a sign of a bigger problem. #Threats #SituationalAwareness

_____

_____

_____

48

You will forget 95% of the concepts you learn if they're not reinforced within seven days, no matter how they are taught or how you learn. #Threats #SituationalAwareness

_____

_____

_____

49

Establishing behavior like ethical decision-making requires more than a one-hour class. It should be practiced on a regular basis. #Threats #SituationalAwareness

_____

_____

_____

50

#Threats are presented and exacerbated differently. As a community leader, CEO, or head of the family, what threats should you consider, and what factors contribute to them?

_____

_____

_____

51

Your goal is to be as proactive as possible when dealing with various #Threats, whether physical, psychological, emotional, or some combination thereof.

_____

_____

_____

52

Continuously learn and apply the skill of #SituationalAwareness so it becomes natural for you at home, in the workplace, and in your community.

_____

_____

_____

53

Developing #SituationalAwareness is a process that takes time. Identifying #Threats and learning how to act on them requires constant practice.

_____

_____

_____

Learn how to #Communicate when under stress. You need #SituationalAwareness skills so you can effectively instruct others when the time comes

Brian Searcy

https://aha.pub/SituationalAwareness

Share the AHA messages from this book socially by going to
https://aha.pub/SituationalAwareness

Scan the QR code or use this link to watch the section videos and more on this section topic:
https://aha.pub/SituationalAwarenessSVs

Section IV

Ten Critical Skills You Need to Have

You'd think that kids or adults are taught everything they need to know in preschool, and then they're primed for life. However, without these ten critical personal skills, they can grow up and live without self-esteem, be easily swayed by the opinions of others, and lack the responsibility to take ownership of their actions.

It is extremely important for you, your family, and your employees to develop these critical skills. Ideally, we would do so from a young age to set us up for success. These critical skills will also help you to learn how to be a good human, not just someone who's trapped in a bubble without regard for what's happening around you.

This section covers ten critical skills you need to have. All of these skills are tied together within the realm of situational awareness and should be observed and exercised on a regular basis. This mindset and behavior born out of these critical personal skills make people more human, something that is often missing in today's world.

54

De-escalating a situation is not a linear approach. Learning #CriticalSkills is a key component of #SituationalAwareness and will help you respond the right way.

_____

_____

_____

55

Being #SelfAware doesn't end with your surroundings. It means knowing what you're capable of and understanding that your actions have an impact. #SituationalAwareness

_____

_____

_____

56

You can follow a process of identifying, assessing, and predicting wherever you go. Are you prepared if something bad happens? #SituationalAwareness

_____

_____

_____

57

There are three elements of being self-aware: knowing what's going on around you, understanding your capabilities, and knowing your actions will have an impact. #SituationalAwareness

_____

_____

_____

58

Being #Perceptive is being aware of things through your sense. When something doesn't seem right, you feel it in your gut. #SituationalAwareness

_____

_____

_____

59

Put your phone away and pay attention to your surroundings. Try that for twenty-one days, and you'll know what normal looks like. Anything else could be a potential threat. #SituationalAwareness

_____

_____

_____

60

Trust your ability to identify things outside the
norm, and develop the ability to act on them.
#SituationalAwareness

_____

_____

_____

61

All animals, including humans, have the innate ability to
sense danger. #SituationalAwareness is a skill you can
hone to help you do just that.

_____

_____

_____

62

Instincts will empower you to act when something happens. Listen to it. #SituationalAwareness

_____

_____

_____

63

Most people listen to respond. They don't listen to learn. You can de-escalate a situation when you #ActivelyListen by asking questions, repeating, and summarizing what you heard. #SituationalAwareness

_____

_____

_____

64

No situation will be exactly what you've planned for. You need critical thinking and learning agility to manage these situations. #SituationalAwareness

_____

_____

_____

65

Too often, people wait for 100 percent of the information before acting. #Decisiveness is being ready to act as the need arises. #SituationalAwareness

---

66

Learn how to #Communicate when under stress. You need #SituationalAwareness skills to effectively instruct others when the time comes.

67

Dr. Noll says, "You can go from calm to angry in ninety seconds." This is especially prevalent on social media, where people routinely fail to recognize how their words affect others. #SituationalAwareness

_____

_____

_____

68

Take responsibility for your own safety. Take care of your community and your neighbors by developing #SituationalAwareness. #Empathy enables you to identify potential threats.

_____

_____

_____

69

In previous generations, safety in the community was everyone's responsibility. To protect yourself and others, you need that same level of kindness and care. #SituationalAwareness

_____

_____

_____

70

You can make your community better and safer by serving and protecting others. #SituationalAwareness

_____

_____

_____

71

Taking responsibility for your own safety is the first step in the process. This will help you take responsibility for all your subsequent actions. #SituationalAwareness

_____

_____

_____

72

More than 75 percent of high school and college graduates don't have well-developed personal skills. Without those skills, you don't understand your responsibilities and can't take responsibility for your actions. #SituationalAwareness

_____

_____

_____

73

To help your children develop #SituationalAwareness, teach them how to communicate and empathize.

_____

_____

_____

74

It's not a school's responsibility to teach #CriticalSkills. It's the parents' responsibility to help their children develop these skills as they grow up. #SituationalAwareness

_____

_____

_____

75

Too many parents act like they're managing a company, using performance metrics. Instead of getting to the root causes, they simply punish children when expectations aren't met.

_____

_____

_____

76

A common culture across the globe is refusing responsibility for one's actions. It's always easiest to blame someone else. #SituationalAwareness

_____

_____

_____

77

We are taught to expect the police or government to fix things for us. When bad things happen, people immediately look for outside help. #SituationalAwareness

_____

_____

_____

78

Many people who call 911 can't describe their situation or even provide their location because they haven't learned to apply #CriticalSkills. #SituationalAwareness

_____

_____

_____

79

You can improve your level of preparedness when faced with threats, which will improve your response. #CriticalSkills #SituationalAwareness

_____

_____

_____

80

Are you managing by metrics or showing leadership within your spheres of influence? Lead by example by demonstrating #CriticalSkills at home, in the workplace, and in the community. #SituationalAwareness

_____

_____

_____

With the proper application of the five-step process of #SituationalAwareness, the potential for becoming a victim decreases dramatically.

Brian Searcy

https://aha.pub/SituationalAwareness

Share the AHA messages from this book socially by going to
https://aha.pub/SituationalAwareness

Scan the QR code or use this link to watch the section videos and more on this section topic:
https://aha.pub/SituationalAwarenessSVs

Section V

Prevent (Identify, Assess, Predict)

To be able to prevent bad things from happening, you need situational awareness and an understanding of the threats we face. In the face of these threats, the likelihood of you, your family, or your employees potentially becoming victims significantly increases without preparation.

This section talks about the first three steps in the five-step process of situational awareness. The five-step process is all about being proactive to prevent threats.

The five-step process of situational awareness is as follows:

1. Identify
2. Assess
3. Predict
4. Remove (Decide)
5. Respond (Act)

Today, all too often, people only train to respond. This thinking is backwards. When we learn how to be proactive to prevent incidents, we are also preparing ourselves to respond by default. That is why the first three steps in the five-step process are the foundation of your situational awareness habits, behaviors, mindset, and process.

We can prevent most bad things from happening, but we cannot prevent everything all of the time. It is best to be prepared and display situational awareness to be proactive instead of reactive in terms of dealing with a problem.

Why is preparation important? Because "Hope Is Not a Strategy." In these unprecedented times, you can't rely on chance to get you out of a bad situation. Your ability to be both proactive and responsive is only as good as your level of planning and preparation.

There are many opportunities now to learn from traditional training, previous experiences, global news, and the Internet. It is crucial that you spend time educating yourself about threats and how to develop a process of situational awareness.

81

The likelihood of you or someone you know becoming a victim increases without preparation. #SituationalAwareness

_____

_____

_____

82

A simple five-step process can prevent you and others from becoming victims: 1) Identify; 2) Assess; 3) Predict; 4) Remove; 5) Respond. Learn #SituationalAwareness.

_____

_____

_____

83

To #Prevent means you have the time and space.
You have the ability to de-escalate a situation.
#SituationalAwareness

_____

_____

_____

84

The first three steps of the five-step process of
#SituationalAwareness will help you decide whether to
respond or remove yourself from the situation.

_____

_____

_____

85

These first three steps put you in a #prepared state and allow you to go about your business while remaining aware of your surroundings. #SituationalAwareness

---

86

To #Identify means assessing your level of concern and whether you feel threatened or not. #SituationalAwareness

---

87

To #Assess means looking for door locks or existing exits if you need to hide or escape. #SituationalAwareness

_____

_____

_____

88

To #Predict is to run scenarios in your head of what may happen and how you might respond. #SituationalAwareness

_____

_____

_____

89

Once you have identified, assessed, and predicted, you are #prepared and ready to act if necessary. You now know if there is anything to prevent. #SituationalAwareness

_____

_____

_____

90

General Eisenhower said, "In preparing for a battle, plans are useless, but planning is indispensable." #SituationalAwareness

_____

_____

_____

91

Military officers always have a plan, but never do they execute the plan exactly as it's written. Critical skills are in place to adapt and enable decision-making. #Prepared #SituationalAwareness

_____

_____

_____

92

More than six million people have bought guns in the United States since January 2020, but most have no idea how to use them. This shows a lack of #SituationalAwareness.

_____

_____

_____

93

Being prepared to carry a weapon is more than just target practice. You need #SituationalAwareness so it can't be taken from or used on you.

_____

_____

_____

94

Imagine the mental health ramifications of pulling the trigger in an active shooter situation. You must know how to carry that weapon so you don't endanger yourself and others. #SituationalAwareness

_____

_____

_____

95

When you're under extreme duress, the only thing you'll be capable of doing is that which you have #prepared for. #SituationalAwareness

_____

_____

_____

96

You need continuing education to take responsibility for yourself and the safety of your community. #Prepared #SituationalAwareness

_____

_____

_____

97

The adage goes, "Hope for the best and #Prepare for the worst." You can proactively stop bad things from happening if you have planned for them. #SituationalAwareness

_____

_____

_____

98

In the U.S. Air Force, everyone learns about the five Ps: Preparation prevents piss-poor performance. Preparation is key. #SituationalAwareness

_____

_____

_____

99

Mark Springer said, "We're living in unprecedented times facing unprecedented threats, so we need to take unprecedented measures to be #prepared." #SituationalAwareness

_____

_____

_____

100

If you're educated on the threats and have developed a process of #SituationalAwareness, you're going to be less anxious, less stressed, and more confident in society.

_____

_____

_____

101

Keep #SituationalAwareness simple. Overcomplicating things, especially under stress, sets you up for failure.

_____

_____

_____

102

With the proper application of the five-step process of #SituationalAwareness, the potential for becoming a victim decreases dramatically. #Prepared

_____

_____

_____

Trust yourself so you can make sound decisions. Don't leave room for doubt. #SituationalAwareness

Brian Searcy

https://aha.pub/SituationalAwareness

Share the AHA messages from this book socially by going to
https://aha.pub/SituationalAwareness

Scan the QR code or use this link to watch the section videos and more on this section topic:
https://aha.pub/SituationalAwarenessSVs

Section VI

Remove (Decide) and Respond (Act)

After discussing the first three steps of the five-step situational awareness process in Section 5, it's time to talk about what comes next.

This section talks about the last two steps of the five-step process: Remove and Respond. These steps are sometimes also referred to as Decide and Act, respectively. In a challenging situation, you need to be prepared to make a critical decision and act accordingly.

It is important to understand that these last two steps are tied to the first three steps of the process. As you practice this process, you will learn how to escalate your levels of awareness based on the situations you find yourself in.

At The Paratus Group, we believe that training people to "just respond" sets them up for failure. When you learn our process to be proactive and prevent things from happening, you also learn how to respond.

This is where the fourth step of the five-step process, remove (or decide), comes into play. The fourth step is for when you need to decide if you're going to prevent or respond. Deciding relies upon the gut feeling—that instinct—that prompts you to choose to remove yourself (or your family) from potentially being hurt. You must trust yourself so you can make sound decisions.

Deciding leads you to the fifth step of the five-step process: responding (or acting). The fifth step is the moment you take action. Your response to a situation will determine your fate and the fate of those around you, so you should be certain of what you want the outcome to be the moment you act. You cannot undo an action, so respond in a way that will not leave you with a feeling of regret.

This section tackles how people at home, in the workplace, or in our communities can potentially interdict when necessary, after careful consideration and preparation. Practical ideas are presented on the proper mindset and behavior when you must pull yourself and others out of a potentially dangerous situation.

103

When you take time to be prepared, you're
ready to act whether something happens or not.
#SItuationalAwareness

_____

_____

_____

104

If you wait until the bad thing happens, it's too late.
#SituationalAwareness

_____

_____

_____

105

A situation is neither positive nor negative. Every situation demands a different response. Just be #SituationallyAware.

_____

_____

_____

106

When you've taken the time to prepare, it will be easier to decide and act. #SituationalAwareness

_____

_____

_____

107

The preparedness that comes with #SituationalAwareness enables you to consider the types of decisions you might have to make based on the real-world factors you are faced with.

_____

_____

_____

108

Training people to "just respond" sets them up for failure. #SituationallyAware

_____

_____

_____

109

When you find yourself in a challenging situation, you must be prepared to make a critical decision and act accordingly. #SituationallyAware

_____

_____

_____

110

To #Decide is the point at which you prevent or respond. It's that gut feeling that makes you remove yourself (or others) to avoid being hurt.

_____

_____

_____

111

The only effective decisions you can make are those you've already considered. They pop into your head when you're under stress, and they could save a life. #SituationalAwareness

_____

_____

_____

112

U.S. Air Force training spends weeks asking, "What if?" to make life-and-death decisions and consider potential consequences.

_____

_____

_____

113

Trust yourself so you can make sound decisions. Don't leave room for doubt. #SituationalAwareness

_____

_____

_____

114

To #Act means you are in the bang. Something is happening—do you run, hide, or fight?

_____

_____

_____

115

You must develop the ability to act on anything outside the norm and trust your ability to not just identify but to act. #SituationalAwareness

_____

_____

_____

116

Are you prepared to get involved and act? What can you do with the training and skills you've developed? #SituationalAwareness

_____

_____

_____

117

Be certain of what you want the outcome to be the moment you act. There's no going back. Respond to situations that will not leave you with a feeling of regret. #SituationalAwareness

_____

_____

_____

118

When you make a decision, you prioritize the action that must be taken. With #SituationalAwareness, these decisions must be made in a timely manner.

_____

_____

_____

119

The actions you take when in a sticky situation should lead you and others out of that situation so no one becomes a victim.

_____

_____

_____

120

Your response to a situation will determine your fate and the fate of those around you. Act based on all the information you've taken in by being #SituationallyAware.

_____

_____

_____

To achieve greater heights in anything, you experience a long and continuous process of learning and #preparation. The decisions you make will impact your life and others'.
#SituationalAwareness

Brian Searcy

https://aha.pub/SituationalAwareness

Share the AHA messages from this book socially by going to
https://aha.pub/SituationalAwareness

Scan the QR code or use this link to watch the section videos and more on this section topic:
https://aha.pub/SituationalAwarenessSVs

Section VII

Life is Better with Preparation

If you are not prepared for the things that might happen, you could put yourself in danger. Having situational awareness gives you the ability to prevent, remove, or respond. It may avert you and those around you from becoming victims.

Today, one out of every two people has levels of stress, anxiety, depression, and loneliness that are affecting their happiness and productivity.

Sadly, many people change the way they live their lives—limiting themselves— because of their lack of situational awareness. Wouldn't it be much better to change the way you live so you're prepared and can take responsibility for your own safety and those around you?

This section concludes with a challenge to you, whether you're the head of the family or a CEO, to continually have a mindset and behavior of situational awareness. Demonstrating situational awareness at all times teaches you how it can greatly improve your mental health and leadership and parenting abilities.

You can continually identify areas in your life where you can promote increased communication, morale, and a culture of taking responsibility wherever you may be. This is ultimately for your own safety and to keep you and others from potentially becoming victims of the kinds of threats we face in our society today.

121

#SituationalAwareness is a perishable skill. You need constant diligence in educating yourself about new and existing threats that can potentially harm your family or your community.

_____

_____

_____

122

Douglas MacArthur said, "Preparedness is the key to success and victory." #SituationalAwareness

_____

_____

_____

123

Louis Pasteur said, "Chance favors the #Prepared mind."
#SituationalAwareness

_____

_____

_____

124

Trust your instincts. They'll let you know when
danger is nearby and allow you to take action.
#SituationalAwareness

_____

_____

_____

125

#Agility is constantly learning agility from mistakes to improve your critical thinking process. #SituationalAwareness

---

126

To #ThinkCritically is not just following a plan or procedure. You can assess and think through different courses of action based on the situation. #SituationalAwareness

---

127

It is best to be #SituationallyAware and #Prepared with no regrets.

_____

_____

_____

128

People of all ages without personal skills have developed bad habits due to distractions like social media and technology. If you don't practice critical skills, you will lose them. #SituationalAwareness

_____

_____

_____

129

You must learn about the need to educate yourself continuously and develop a consistent mindset that eventually becomes second nature to you. #SituationalAwareness

_____

_____

_____

130

Even during a pandemic, you can dramatically improve your mental health and the ability to respond to threats if you put in the time to be prepared. #SituationalAwareness

_____

_____

_____

131

You may not know exactly what will happen, but you are prepared to deal with anything that comes your way. #SituationalAwareness helps you avoid saying, "I regret not doing that."

_____

_____

_____

132

The last thing you ever want is to know you have a potential solution to a potential threat but have not prepared those around you to respond. #SituationalAwareness

_____

_____

_____

133

#SituationalAwareness should be as natural to you as breathing.

134

In your career, you constantly train and refresh your mind and body to stay #prepared. You should have the same mindset when life happens. #SituationalAwareness

135

When you practice #SituationalAwareness on a regular basis, you are prepared for what you hope never happens. Whatever it is, you're prepared. #SituationalAwareness

_____

_____

_____

136

You must be available and ready when presenting solutions so the people around you are prepared to deal with a potential threat. #SituationalAwareness

_____

_____

_____

137

You build a strong foundation of #SituationalAwareness by being prepared. It allows you to be proactive so you can respond to life as it happens.

_____

_____

_____

138

When you stay on top of being #SituationallyAware, you can make decisions based on educated training, critical thinking, and common sense—not fear.

_____

_____

_____

139

To achieve greater heights in anything, you experience a long and continuous learning and preparation process. The decisions you make will impact your life and others'.
#SituationalAwareness

_____

_____

_____

140

#SituationalAwareness is not "one and done." It is a process of always staying on top of things with a consistency of learning to be prepared.

_____

_____

_____

About the Author

Brian Searcy, a retired U.S. Air Force Colonel, is the founder and CEO of The Paratus Group, where he uses his decades-tested and decorated senior leadership career and military training to solve the need for relevant and effective principles in leadership. He provides training methodologies and programs for the learning of situational awareness. His vision for the company is to "Redefine How Safety is Learned" to make schools, churches, the workplace, and communities as safe as possible.

His revolutionary training on situational awareness has helped many learn how to be true first responders and taught many individuals, families, and work personnel to be "prepared to survive."